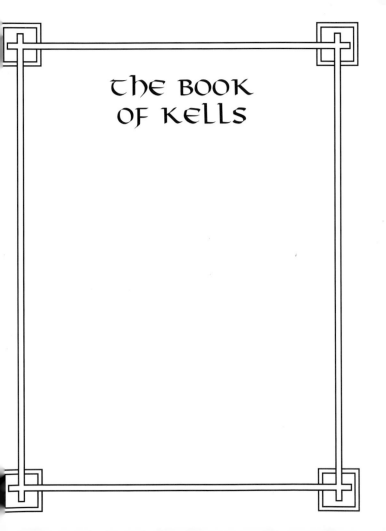

THE BOOK
OF KELLS

By Harry Adès

Designed by Tony and Penny Mills

THE BOOK OF KELLS

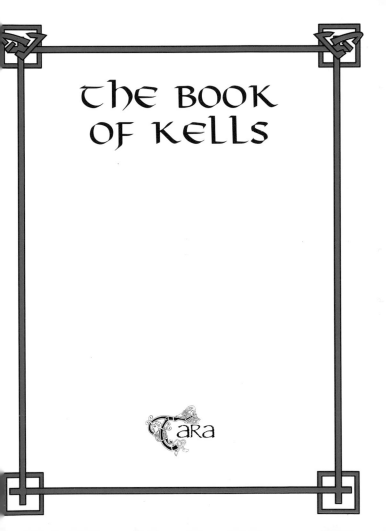

Tara

This edition published and distributed by Tara, 1999

Tara is an imprint of Parragon

Parragon
Queen Street House
4 Queen Street
Bath BA1 1HE

Produced by Magpie Books, an imprint of
Robinson Publishing Ltd, London

ISBN 1 90287 906 6

A copy of the British Library Cataloguing-in-Publication Data is
available from the British Library

Printed in China

CONTENTS

vi

INTRODUCTION

THE *Book of Kells* is one of the world's greatest illuminated manuscripts. It consists of the four gospels of the New Testament, which tell the story of Christ's life, written in Latin in beautifully rounded script. The text of such manuscripts was adorned with colours, tracery and pictures, but the *Book of Kells* is unsurpassed for the exquisite quality of its decoration and its abundance of curious figures, animals and intricate abstract shapes. Interspersed in its text are pages entirely devoted to the ornamentation of a few letters or words, or to portraits of gospel characters or scenes, all magnificent works of art with the finest and most imaginative designs. Originally bound in a golden cover encrusted with gems, the

(Opposite) folio 27v The Evangelical Symbols

1

book would have been the monastery's most precious possession. It was too precious for everyday use and was displayed on the altar for festive occasions.

No one is sure when or where the book was written. Some say it was begun just before 797 AD by St Columba's loyal monks to celebrate the second centenary of his death. Others think that its sublime artistry, using elements from many sources, points to a later date. Whatever is true, the uncertainty only adds to the sense of wonder and mystery that surround it.

The *Book of Kells* has survived remarkably well. It has only lost around thirty of its 370 pages, an extraordinary outcome considering the Viking attacks, its theft and burial in the earth, the persistent raiding of the Danes and the ravages of well over a thousand years.

In this book we learn of the different artists and their visions of the world. We

(Opposite) folio 5r

2

3

meet the four masters and immerse ourselves in their genius. We explore some of the most beautiful illuminations ever painted. We search for meaning in the arcane symbols and themes woven into the illustrations. We delve into the life of the scribes and uncover the secrets of their calling. Above all we see why the *Book of Kells* is a lasting symbol of Irish creativity and a unique work of art.

history

OR all the dazzling brilliance of the *Book of Kells*, its history is only patchy and obscure. The origin of such manuscripts is notoriously hard to trace, as they were easily and often moved from monastery to monastery without record. The *Book of Kells* troubles historians even further, owing to its missing colophon, the all-important final page inscribed with details of authorship and location.

The first mention of its existence is in the Annals of Ulster, which tell how, in 1007, the manuscript, "the chief treasure of the western world" was "wickedly stolen in the night" from the monastery at Kells, only to be recovered a few months later from under a sod of earth. The thieves had torn it from its gold and jewel-bedecked cover, which was never seen again. They probably tossed the priceless manuscript aside like a bundle of old rags. In reality, the book dates from about 200 years before this incident, and the story surrounding its early years is no less dramatic.

Although no one can be sure, it is widely believed that the *Book of Kells* was started at a monastery founded by St Columba on the Scottish island of Iona. St Columba, sometimes known as Columcille (Columb of the Church), was born in the north-west of Ireland around 521. We know that the *Book of Kells* is connected to him, as it is referred to in the Annals as "the great Gospel of Columcille".

The ancient chronicles say Columba was entitled to be the King of Ireland, but he spurned the luxuries and power of royalty to lead the hard and comfortless life of a monk devoted to God. At 32, he founded a monastery at Durrow in the centre of Ireland, and another at Derry. But the strength of his calling drove him from Ireland. He wanted to spread God's word to the wider world. Like a stepping-stone between Britain and Ireland, tiny Iona, only three-and-a-half miles long and half a mile wide, came to be one of his most influential monasteries. From here, Christianity spread in all directions. He converted the Anglo-Saxons of northern England and the Picts of Scotland; his faith even reached Iceland hundreds of miles away.

The Irish monasteries were becoming great centres of learning and cultivation, and Iona was no exception. Columba was a keen scribe and put into motion the long-standing practice of writing and copying the holy scriptures in his monasteries. Of course, in those days every book had to be written by hand and monks sat for hours on end poring over the text and scrutinizing the designs of other books.

Around the time of Columba's death in 597, Irish missionaries had started to evangelize on the continent. Amongst the monasteries they built, that of St Gall's at Bobbio in northern Italy was one of the most important. For it was here that the Irish monks first saw the illuminated manuscripts of the Copts, Christians of Egypt, with their beautiful interlacing designs and dotted decorations. Soon these ideas were adopted and developed to extraordinary levels by the Irish artists.

The ideas of the eastern texts blended perfectly with the distinctive Celtic designs, as can be seen in the great manuscripts of the seventh and eighth centuries, such as the *Book of Durrow*, the *Book of Lichfield* and the *Book of Lindisfarne*. These books already display immense skill and artistry.

The *Book of Kells* belongs to the tradition of these earlier manuscripts, but it is far more than a simple continuation of the line. It is the crowning achievement of the Irish illuminators, never matched before or since. Its decoration is more imaginative and fanciful, its designs more intricate, given to stunning detail, and its whole

(Opposite) folio 29r The opening of St Matthew's Gospel

concept more visionary than any other manuscript. In short, it was the supreme accomplishment of the Irish artists.

Judging by the ornamentation of the books of this period, we can place the *Book of Kells* between the late eighth and early ninth centuries. It belongs to the style of the northern monasteries, in particular those associated with St Columba, hence its connection to Iona. The natural question now is: how did it get to Kells?

In 805, Viking raiders came in their longboats to Iona to loot the monastery of its gold and silver. The pagans showed no respect for human life nor the sanctity of the monastery. They massacred sixty-eight monks and stripped the buildings of their holy objects, melting them down into coins. The surviving monks fled, clutching their precious Gospels close to them and sailed in their little boats back to Ireland. At Kells (Ceananas Mór, forty miles north-west of

(Opposite) folio 129v Evangelical Symbols

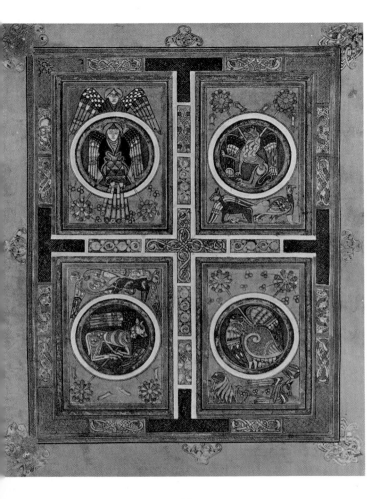

Dublin) they set up a new monastery and settled down once again to complete the manuscript.

At least that was their hope, but calamity was never far away, for a short period of peace was followed by years of upheaval. Throughout the tenth century Kells was sacked and plundered repeatedly, this time by Danish invaders. How the great book survived, nobody knows; the monks had probably made hiding-places for it in the thick stone walls. The manuscript, however, was never completed. Some pages are altogether blank, while others have only one colour and borders still waiting to be filled with minute interweaving ribbons. We can only assume that by then the great illuminators had died, while the turmoil of the raids and invasions had made it impossible for them to pass on their knowledge to their successors.

For centuries the unfinished manuscript was kept and revered at Kells (except for the short interlude when it was stolen), until the mid-seventeenth century. By that time the monastery, which had then become a church, was in such a state of disrepair that it was used not for worship, but as a horses' stable. Around 1653, during the strife of the Cromwellian period, the governor of Kells sent the book to Trinity College in Dublin for safety. There it has remained ever since. Sadly, having escaped destruction at the hands of the Vikings and Danes, it suffered its worst catastrophe here. In about 1820, an incompetent bookbinder carelessly trimmed away the edges of the decoration on many pages. Nonetheless, the *Book of Kells* is still a wonderful sight, and now housed in the Long Room of Trinity College library, everyone is free to enjoy its splendour.

MATERIALS

THE *Book of Kells* once had around 370 folios, in other words 740 pages, but only 340 folios have survived. They are vellum leaves, made of high quality calf-skin. A mixture of lime and excrement was used to remove the hairs of the skin. The pelt was then strung across a wooden frame so that lumps of flesh and fur could be scraped away with a knife. Then the hide was stretched and flattened, and smoothed with a pumice stone. The resulting vellum made an excellent medium for their art. After it had been cut to size, it was measured for text and pricks were made at regular intervals in the margins, between which guidelines would have been scored. It was then ready for use.

The estimate is that the skins of around

(Opposite) folio 188r. The beginning of St Luke's Gospel

185 calves were needed to make the *Book of Kells*. If the book was produced in a short space of time, it has been suggested that there must have been a herd of more than 1200 animals to make this possible. Only the very wealthiest places could afford such herds. Perhaps several monasteries would share their skins, especially for the making of such a luxury book.

All monasteries farmed animals for food. Geese were particularly useful to the scribes as they provided eggs, which were used to bind the pigments, and their feathers made excellent quills. The Portrait of St John (folio 291v) shows the evangelist holding a colourful version of a quill in his right hand. By his right foot, there is an ink-pot too. Most were made from cow's horns and stuck in the earth by one's feet, to keep them from spilling on the page.

The inks and pigments were all naturally occurring. Inks of various qualities were

(Opposite) folio 291v

used. The brownish-looking one was made from an iron compound ground together with crushed oak apples. Soot was used for the jet black ink.

The artists could play with a spectrum of colours: many more than in earlier Celtic manuscripts. But many pigments were extremely difficult to come by. Scientists have pinpointed the ingredients of most, but the exact combinations of several remain a mystery. The yellow, so generously applied to the Chi-Rho page, was a mineral (yellow arsenic sulphide) found in Irish soil. It was called orpiment, meaning gold pigment, and made a good cheap substitute for the real thing. The green was derived from copper, while several types of blue came from the plants of northern Europe. Red lead was used for the bright reds, as found in the Portrait of Christ. The darker red was a far more exotic product made from the pregnant body of a Mediterranean insect, known as "kermes", which the Romans believed to be a berry.

Perhaps the rarest and most sparingly-used colour was the brilliant blue obtained from the precious stone *lapis lazuli*. Amazingly, at that time it came from only one known place, a faraway mine in the inhospitable mountains of north-east Afghanistan. It must have been shockingly expensive and probably came to Ireland only in the smallest quantities.

The vibrant colours of the manuscript are difficult to reproduce exactly, and although every effort has been made with the images in this book, the true colours of the *Book of Kells* are best appreciated by viewing the original pages at Trinity College, Dublin.

inside the book of kells

THE *Book of Kells* never fails to impress those who see it. The decoration is so lavish, so colourful and so original, embellished with innumerable designs, like baffling interlacing knots or battling beasts or sprouting tendrils, that sometimes it is hard to imagine how it was created. In several instances the interweaving threads are so small that they are barely visible without a magnifying glass. Even so, they are woven together so perfectly and with such regimental precision that it is almost impossible to see where one begins and another ends. To the people of the Middle Ages it was a holy book in every sense. Not only was it the sacred word of the gospels,

(Opposite) Initial letters from copies by Helen Campbell D'Olier

Q

R

Q

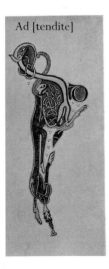

Ad [tendite]

ET

AD

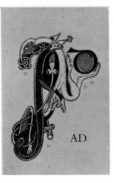

AI

AT i[lli]

nor just an object of high veneration in the monastery. Its decoration was so exquisite that it was thought to be the work of angels.

Of course, it had earthly origins and followed a scheme typical of all the manuscripts at that time. It mainly consists of the Latin text of the gospels, written in a style known as "insular majuscule" on leaves of vellum about 13½ by 9½ inches in size. Each gospel was introduced by a page of evangelical symbols (Matthew is represented by a winged man, Mark a winged lion, Luke a winged ox, and John by an eagle), a portrait of the evangelist, and rich ornamentation of the opening words or letters of the gospel. Preceding them were "etymologies" of Hebrew names; canon tables, which displayed the similarities between the gospels; short summaries of the events in each gospel, known as *Breves causae*; and the *Argumenta*, descriptions of the evangelists.

The artists of the *Book of Kells* brought incredible ingenuity to the rendering of this scheme. Not a single drawing is repeated and no idea overused in its seemingly endless stream of figures, forms and decoration. Its great fusion of styles and its overall variety strongly suggest that more than one artist was involved in its creation. In fact, it would have been the joint effort of many hands over many years.

Monks would have worked together in a scriptorium, the part of the monastery specially reserved for writing. The great masters would have been helped by several apprentices, who carried out the less difficult tasks. The most complicated and beautiful pages were painted on loose leaves, so that artists could work on them at any time and then add them to the book later. Several of these pages must have been entrusted to one artist in particular. Françoise Henry's study of the *Book of Kells* has revealed at least four master illuminators. She calls them the Goldsmith, the Portrait Painter, and the Illustrator. The last she leaves unnamed, but he has a youthful, playful touch, so we could call him the Joker.

The Goldsmith

The Goldsmith's pages are perhaps the most breathtaking of the entire book. His works are indeed treasures, but he gets his name from his abstract designs that resemble those wrought in precious metals at that time. He also has a fondness for the colours of deep yellow gold and a flashing silvery blue. Each of his pages demonstrates exceptional technical mastery and an artistic vision that builds minute details into a beautifully-conceived whole.

There is only one "carpet page" in the *Book of Kells*, a page devoted entirely to abstract decoration (which was an idea borrowed from the Coptic texts of the east). It is painted by the Goldsmith. Each gospel would probably have had its own carpet page, but they have been lost.

Known as the Eight-Circled Cross (folio 33r) this carpet page is a splendid example

(Opposite) folio 33r

of delicate and balanced ornamentation. Although the overall design is symmetrical, no motif or pattern of knotwork is doubled. At first glance our eyes seem to find repetition everywhere, but the illusion melts away the longer we look. Often the differences are as subtle as an alternative arrangement of colour, or the sudden change in the direction of a curve. So the Goldsmith achieves the appearance of a limitless vocabulary of designs.

At the ends and intersections of the cross, the eight circles are filled with swirling spirals and triskeles (three-legged shapes within a circle). Similar forms appear on jewellery and metalwork of about that time, most noticeably the Tara Brooch, on view in the National Museum of Ireland, Dublin.

Following the Eight-Circled Cross is the most famous page in the *Book of Kells*. It has also been described as "the most elaborate page of calligraphy ever executed". The

(Opposite) folio 34r

hgeneratio

27

Monogram or Chi-Rho page (folio 34r) consists of just three abbreviated words, but is comprised of almost every design found in Celtic art. The phrase XRI B GENERATIO (Christi autem generatio), meaning "Now the birth of Jesus Christ", comes from the beginning of Matthew's account of the nativity (Matthew 1 v.18). The page is, therefore, a joyous celebration of Christ's birth, a trumpeting of God's presence among us, and a jubilation of all life on Earth.

Not surprisingly, the illumination is absolutely teeming. Amongst the spirals that seem to wind to infinity, between the unfathomable knots of thread and interlaces of ribbon, around the circles and triskeles that bound off the page, are countless, often barely perceptible, animals, birds, beasts, snakes, insects, humans and angels. Take the page's focus, the great diamond intersection of the sweeping strokes of the X, the Greek letter "chi". In this tiny space alone are four humans, four animals, twelve birds, and a number of slithering vipers. Nearby, two moths adorn a chrysalis, a symbol of the cycle of life and rejuvenation. At the foot of the page cats and mice play together with what looks to be a portion of communion bread, owing to a small cross on its surface. Some have taken this to represent the biblical proverb "The wolf shall also dwell with the lamb", from the Book of Isaiah. To the right of the cats, an otter gnaws happily on a fish. Even the P, the Greek letter "rho" (chi and rho making up the first two letters of Christ), sprouts a human head. Life is celebrated everywhere.

The Goldsmith is also credited with three of the four folios (29r, 130r, 292r) that feature the opening words of the gospels. The beginning of St John's Gospel (folio 292r) has a particularly beguiling and intelligent design. The words are "In principio erat verbum et verbum", meaning "In the beginning was the word and the word (was God)". Notice how the N is constructed with the two inside halves of the main vertical bars. They are more

deeply coloured to set them apart. The I and P are made up of the remaining halves. It is amazing how these opening letters appear as a single diminishing unit (a technique known as *diminuendo*), their tops and bottoms brought together by four sets of four revolving circles, or roundels. The Goldsmith's grace and intricacy can be seen in threads and biting snake-like beasts in the "RINCI" section. The final I is formed by a man who seems to play on a harp made by the C next to him. Actually the "harp" is a beast, a bird and a reptile, while the man's fingers resemble the harp's strings.

(Opposite) folio 292r

The Portrait Painter

If the Goldsmith was the master of visual
trickery and abstract flights of fancy, then it
was left to the Portrait Painter to lend
gravity and realism to the *Book of Kells*. His
three portraits, one of St Matthew (folio
28v), of St John (folio 291v), and of a figure
taken to be either Christ, Luke or Mark
(folio 32v), have been called the most
impressive effigies ever designed by an Irish
artist. The portrait of St Matthew (folio
28v), for instance, has all the solemnity one
would expect from such a holy and ven-
erated manuscript. St Matthew stands
barefoot before us, his eyes wide and full of
righteousness, his robe cascading about him
in generous folds of gold and purple, while
in his left hand he parades his Gospel.
Behind him a sumptuous velvet throne is
flanked by the symbols of the other
evangelists. A scarlet halo surrounds his

(Opposite) folio 28v

locks of golden hair. It is a majestic portrait.

Made up of numerous intertwining beasts, the border proves that the Portrait Painter was also no slouch at ornamentation. He lacks, however, the virtuosity of the Goldsmith, and we feel that he certainly gets more pleasure from drawing figures.

The next portrait in the book is sunk in controversy. The so-called Doubtful Portrait (folio 32v) has many similarities to the pictures of John and Matthew, so some have presumed that it is one of the missing portraits of Luke or Mark. However, important characteristics of the portrait suggest that it is of Christ. Firstly, the page comes between the genealogy of Christ and the Chi-Rho Monogram page, which celebrates Christ's birth. In this context there seems no reason why it should be an evangelist.

This belief is strengthened further when one considers the imagery on the page.

(Opposite) folio 32v

34

Where the others have haloes, this figure has a cross; and in no other portrait is the central figure accompanied by angels. Most convincing, though, is the inclusion of peacocks, chalices and vines around the figure's flaxen hair. The chalices and vines have been taken to denote eucharistic wine, while the peacock has long symbolized the incorruptibility of Christ. This is because it was thought to have flesh so hard that it would never rot. The notion was tested by St Augustine of Hippo, who, one day, decided to leave a scrap of his roast peacock out in the sun. After a month, the scrap had not even begun to smell. A year later, the flesh was only slightly dehydrated.

Imagery of this sort occurs frequently in the *Book of Kells*, often by means of little figures or animals running between the lines of text, or slipping almost unseen into the exuberant decoration. On this page too, peacocks form part of the ornamentation in the bars each side of Christ, and in two of the semi-circles that stick out at either side.

The Illustrator

No artist of the *Book of Kells* is as wild as the Illustrator. This driven and erratic character paints with a raw energy that explodes into his designs. He does not care for the daintiness of minute and intricate decoration, nor does he have the patience to carry it out. He puts no value in the refinement of a perfectly-ordered frame. His taste for colour is brash, often splashing brilliant green next to dusky red, its opposite. Despite this, perhaps because of this, his pictures are among the most vivid, most visionary of all. Umberto Eco, the Italian novelist and philosopher, described the *Book of Kells* as "the product of a cold-blooded hallucination". This applies to no one's work better than the Illustrator.

He depicted dramatic incidents from Christ's life, such as the Temptation and the Arrest, the first ever pictures of such scenes in manuscripts of this kind. Even in the gentle image of the Virgin and Child (folio

37

7v) there is evidence of his dynamism. The design has no neat focus to it: the eyes of the angels that surround the Madonna tend to take our attention away from, rather than directing it to her. Six curious figures placed on the border, staring away from Christ and Mary, unsettle us further. The Virgin's throne is topped off with the head of some rapacious monster, whose slavering tongue coils and knots around the back of the chair. Compared to the austere work of the Portrait Painter, this picture fizzes with life. Accuracy is not the Illustrator's main concern, as indicated by the Madonna's two right feet, and Christ's two left feet and two left hands.

Another of his pieces, folio 124r, is a sequence of text. Typically, this artist has chosen one of the most dramatic moments in the gospels, the Crucifixion, taken from Matthew 27v.38. The capital T of Tunc crucifixerant ("then they crucified") is a

(Opposite) folio 7v

39

fearsome lion, whose burning red tongue entwines with horned serpents. The image arouses a horror appropriate for the barbaric deaths it introduces. The words "XPI cum eo duos latrones", "Christ and with him two thieves" are set into the shape of a cross, impressing the scene on our minds. In those days, the gospels had not been divided into verses, so such illuminations helped the readers around the text. On the border, similar to the picture of the Virgin and Child, the Illustrator has drawn three curious groups of people. Each figure stares unblinkingly with one great eye, perhaps a representation of the crowd beholding the scene with terror. Even though the page is only script, the Illustrator, with his custom-ary flourish, has injected it with life.

(Opposite) folio 124r

41

The Joker

The *Book of Kells* is one of the most important religious manuscripts ever written, but its illustrations are often far from austere. There are no actual jokes in the text as such, but many of the pictures have an unexpected wit.

The Joker is the hand behind many of these, gracing the pages with a sense of humour both gentle and endearing. In one instance he draws a monk riding horseback over a word, while above him the finishing stroke of a letter forms his tonsure. He also enlivens the many pages of otherwise pure text with his drawings of animals, including cats, hens, cocks, doves, goats, greyhounds, hares and a lizard.

The Joker was not responsible for any of the grand ornamental pages, but there are signs of his collaboration with the other artists throughout the book. He seems to

(Opposite) folio 130r

have worked in particular with the Goldsmith. The opening page to St Mark's Gospel (folio 130r) is clearly another of the Goldsmith's masterpieces. But look at the figure, probably St Mark, in the top right corner. A lion that has taken form from the border attempts to clamp its jaws on him. St Mark is too clever for him. He grips the beast's tongue firmly in his hand and escapes danger. This quirky scene is the Joker's touch.

Remember the cats and mice at the bottom of the Monogram page, or the moths, or the otter and the fish? These too are the Joker's. We have the sense of a man who took pleasure in the simple things around him, who would stroll into the monastery yard and watch the animals at play, perhaps sketching them on to wax tablets. Such happy drawings help to ground the other-worldly universe of the *Book of Kells* in everyday life.

The five-page sequence of the Genealogy of Christ, three of which are reproduced

(Opposite) folio 200r

facta est uox filius meus dilectus me-
bene — complacuit mihi

Ipse ihesus incipiens quasi annorum triginta ut putabatur filius

ioseph
qui fuit heli
qui fuit matha
qui fuit leui
qui fuit melchi
qui fuit iannae
qui fuit ioseph
qui fuit mathat hie
qui fuit amos
qui fuit nauum
qui fuit esli
qui fuit nagge
qui fuit enaud

here (folios 200r–201r) is one of the most charming sections of the manuscript. The pages list Christ's ancestors all the way from Joseph to Abraham to Adam to God.

What could have been a dull procession of names, the Joker transforms wonderfully, simply by linking each line of text. The capital Q of every "Qui fuit" – and there are over seventy – meaning "who was the son of" loops into the one below it. In this way, the illustrations are a kind of pictorial symbol for the text that they accompany: a long and connected line of life.

But the most pleasing aspect of this section is the subtle world conjured up in the capital letters. This seemingly chaotic burst of lines and colour is in fact a marvellous little story. At the head of the list is a bearded man, perhaps the Gene-alogy's metaphorical father figure. Below him, creatures sprawl in a terrible mass of tangled limbs, creating in their confusion

(Opposite) folio 200v

Ui	fuit	enachad
Ui	fuit	icce
Ui	fuit	semei
Ui	fuit	ioseph·osse
Ui	fuit	iuda
Ui	fuit	iohanna
Ui	fuit	ressa
Ui	fuit	zorbba
Ui	fuit	salachiel
Ui	fuit	Heri
Ui	fuit	melchi
Ui	fuit	addi
Ui	fuit	cosum
Ui	fuit	elmadam
Ui	fuit	er
Ui	fuit	iesu
Ui	fuit	eliezer

the parade of linked Q's. Each is made of a dog's twisted and elongated body. Animals contorting into the shapes of letters are called "zoomorphic" letters. Meanwhile, birds are trapped in the middle of every Q, and struggle to free themselves.

On the first page, in their efforts to flee, they stretch their unprotected necks into the margins, easy bait for the ravenous hounds. The birds at the bottom of the page are faring a little better, as the dogs' teeth grapple and slip over their hard, shiny beaks. Over the page the tide is turning in the birds' favour. Cunningly, they strain their necks so far that they wrap into indigestible knots. Some have managed to outmanoeuvre the dogs, who stare into space, outwitted. By the final page the birds have wrested themselves from the frenzy altogether, leaving the dogs to fight and bite each other. They stand resplendent in the triumph of peace, their wings ablaze with colour.

(Opposite) folio 201r

fuit	zorim
fuit	macchat
fuit	leui
fuit	semeon
fuit	iuda
fuit	ioseph
fuit	iona
fuit	eliacim
fuit	melcha
fuit	menna
fuit	macchachia
fuit	nathan
fuit	dauid
fuit	iesse
fuit	obed
fuit	boos
fuit	salmon

The last two pages of the Genealogy were completed by an inferior artist, and the complicated interweaving of the letters has been abandoned.

As with the Illustrator's "Tunc crucifixerant" page, many of the Joker's drawings enhance the meaning of the text. There are two particularly striking instances of this. The first, at Luke 16v.13, involves the text "Nemo servus potest duobus dominis servire" meaning "no servant can serve two masters". The N of Nemo consists of two contorting men, supposedly the masters in question, each tugging aggressively on the other's beard. The second is for the parable of the sower, which has a cock and two hens strutting and pecking for stray seeds between the lines of text. For those who could not read and did not know any Latin, pictures such as these must have been crucial to understand the gospels and the Christian message.

The Scribes and their text

It is not clear whether the scribes – the writers of the text – were the same people as the artists or not. At least four scribes have been identified from the different styles of handwriting and adornments. In some instances, however, such as in folio 104r, it is pretty clear that the scribe was responsible for all the features on the page: text, initials and decoration.

No other manuscript of that time shows such desire to brighten pages of the text with so many illuminated initials, drawings and splashes of colour as the *Book of Kells*. This page is a perfect example, employing so many different devices to entrance the reader. It has decorated initials, several zoo-morphic letters, all of course unique, an angular capital (seen in the second initial from the top), coloured letters, flowery punctuation, and an illustration of a bird to balance a line. In the fourth and fifth lines from the bottom, tiny cross-hatchings over the XPS and XPI indicate the shortened forms of Christ. A similar device was used for the word "Jesus", which was often abbreviated to IHS with a fish drawn above it. This was because each letter of *ichthys*, the Greek word for fish, was the first letter of the words in the phrase "Jesus Christ Son of God Saviour".

Folio 104r is a taste of the variety and vitality of the *Book of Kells*. The scribes were never content to regurgitate old initials, and they produced more different forms than in any other Celtic manuscript. In the two types of illuminated initials in the book, the decorated black letters and the zoomorphic (animal) alphabet, nearly all of the Latin alphabet is represented. For this reason, the *Book of Kells* is the principal source of letter-forms for calligraphers across the world.

The scribes seem infinitely resourceful. Sometimes only one animal is used, its long sinuous body pulled and pushed into the

(Opposite) folio 104r

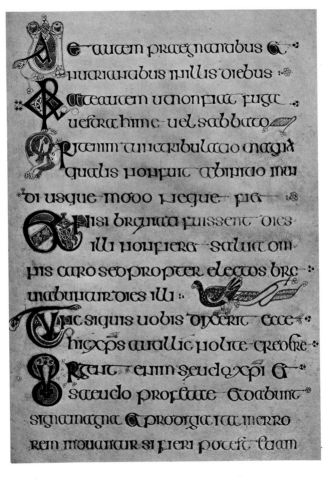

Ae autem praegnatibus et
nutriantibus in illis diebus ÷

Rate autem ut non fiat fuga
uestra hieme uel sabbato

Rit enim tunc tribulatio magna
qualis non fuit ab initio mun
di usque modo neque fiet

Et nisi breuiata fuissent dies
illi non fieret salua om
nis caro sed propter electos bre
uiabuntur dies illi ÷

Tunc siquis uobis dixerit ecce
hic xps aut illic nolite credere

Surgent enim pseudoxpi et
pseudo profetae et dabunt
signa magna et prodigia ita ut erro
rem inducantur si fieri potest etiam

53

required figure, with only the odd claw or a tiny mouth giving it away. The more ambitious capitals employ two or more animals. Often they writhe about one another, tongues spilling out into exuberant decoration to complete the letter. On occasion they attack, and their bodies locked in battle make up the form.

With such regular fine rounded letters, the scribes went to great lengths to ensure that their script was neat. Of course, mistakes were bound to happen. Where a word had been left out, for example, the scribes would introduce it in the script in small letters between the lines, sometimes guarded between the legs of a ferocious beast, or shielded under the wing of a bird. If a word had been repeated, they showed this by discreetly putting little dots inside the letters. Minor errors could be scraped out of the vellum with a knife.

(Opposite) Initial letters from copies by Helen Campbell D'Olier.

AV

ET DIXit

PO[nite]

Pa(ter)

A[pparuit]

ID

AS

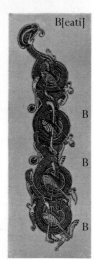

B[eati]

B

B

B

55

They hated leaving a line half-full and had several techniques to disguise this awkwardness. One, as we have seen, was to fill the gap with a bird or a fish, or a winding set of colourful scrolls. Another they called "turn-in-the-path" or "head-under-wing", where they continued the writing from the line below in the space left above. These fillers often had animal decoration next to them. This can be seen three times on folio 19v, the first time marked by a lion and the others by square-and-cross shaped ornaments.

The life of a scribe was a difficult one. They spent many hours stooped over their desks, in an often cold and dark scriptorium, attending to the painstaking detail of their work. Full concentration was needed, not to mention an unfaltering flow of creative energy. In some earlier manuscripts, though not in the *Book of Kells*, the monks wrote their feelings in the margins of the text. One wondered why if he only used three fingers

(Opposite) folio 19v

exponatur uescendi desiderio collocato &
quaerentibus fructus laboris & domagiste-
rii docarina serutur

riae sacerdoti appa-
ruit angelus & adnuntauit ei filium iohan
nem & idem mariae adnuntauit angelus
filium ihm toribus & uaca.
Natiuitatem ihu adnuntiat angelus pas
pic simeon puerum ihm & benedicat
oin & adeuna profetassa bat
& annorum duodecim ihs intemplo doce-
seniores usmum poenitez
Ubi iohannis baptizat populum bap.

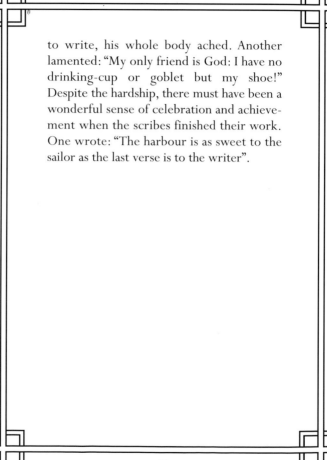

to write, his whole body ached. Another lamented: "My only friend is God: I have no drinking-cup or goblet but my shoe!" Despite the hardship, there must have been a wonderful sense of celebration and achievement when the scribes finished their work. One wrote: "The harbour is as sweet to the sailor as the last verse is to the writer".